A Reformer's Journey: The Martin Luther Story

Martin Luther, the 16th-century German monk, priest, professor, and theologian, is a pivotal figure in the history of Christianity and Western civilization. His life and work laid the foundation for the Protestant Reformation, reshaping the religious, social, and political landscape of his time. This short biography explores the life of Martin Luther delving into his early years, upbringing, and the events that led to his pivotal role in the Reformation.

On November 10, 1483, in the small town of Eisleben, in the Holy Roman Empire, Hans and Margarethe Luther welcomed their son, Martin, into the world. The Luthers were of modest means, and Hans, his father, was a miner by trade. His early years were marked by a strict and disciplined upbringing, as was common in the 15th century. His parents instilled in him a strong work ethic and a deep sense of religious devotion.

Luther's journey towards becoming a prominent religious figure began with his education. At the age of seven, he attended a local school in Mansfeld, where he learned the basics of reading, writing, and arithmetic. His intellectual prowess was evident from an early age, and he was sent to the Latin school in Magdeburg, where he received a classical education that would prove crucial in his later theological pursuits.

In 1501, at the age of 17, Luther began his university studies at the University of Erfurt. He initially studied law, as his father had hopes of him becoming a lawyer. However, a life-altering event occurred in 1505, when Luther was caught in a violent thunderstorm and, fearing for his life, made a vow to become a monk if he survived. He miraculously survived the storm and, true to his vow, he entered the Augustinian monastery in Erfurt.

Luther's time in the monastery was marked by rigorous religious practice and deep contemplation. He followed the strict Augustinian rule, dedicating himself to prayer, fasting, and self-mortification. In this environment, he sought spiritual solace and answers to his profound theological questions.

Luther's superiors recognized his intellectual potential and decided to send him to the University of Wittenberg to further his studies. There, he delved into theology and philosophy, earning his bachelor's and doctoral degrees. His academic pursuits led him to explore the writings of the Church Fathers and classical philosophers, fostering a deep intellectual curiosity that would shape his future as a theologian.

The Fateful Pilgrimage to Rome

In 1510, Luther embarked on a pilgrimage to Rome, a journey that was intended to deepen his spiritual understanding and commitment. However, the trip had a profound impact on him, as he was disillusioned by the corruption and moral decay he observed within the Catholic Church during his visit to the heart of Christendom. This experience would plant the seeds of his later challenges to the Church's practices and doctrines.

The turning point in Martin Luther's life and the spark that ignited the Reformation came on October 31, 1517, when he famously posted his "95 Theses" on the door of the Castle Church in Wittenberg. In these theses, Luther criticized the sale of indulgences, a common practice in the Catholic Church, and called for a theological debate on the subject. Luther's actions were not intended to divide the Church but to reform what he saw as corrupt practices. However, this act of defiance set off a chain of events that would forever change the Christian world.

As Luther's influence grew, so did the opposition from the Catholic Church. In 1520, Pope Leo X issued a papal bull threatening Luther with excommunication if he did not recant his views. Luther's response was to publicly burn the papal bull, and in 1521, he was summoned to the Diet of Worms, an imperial assembly where he was called upon to renounce his beliefs. Luther's response, "Here I stand; I can do no other," marked his unwavering commitment to his convictions, despite the potential consequences.

Luther's ideas quickly gained traction, thanks in part to the recent invention of the printing press, which allowed for the rapid dissemination of his writings. His call for the Bible to be made available to the common people in their own language was particularly revolutionary. His translation of the New Testament into German in 1522 marked a significant step in this direction. His followers, known as Lutherans, grew in number, and his influence extended beyond Germany.

Luther's teachings inspired not only religious reform but also social and political change. In 1525, the Peasants' War broke out in Germany, and some of the peasants looked to Luther for support. While Luther sympathized with their grievances, he opposed the violence and chaos of the rebellion. He also experienced personal change during this time, marrying Katharina von Bora, a former nun, in 1525, thereby challenging the traditional celibacy of the clergy.

Luther's theology and ideas were codified in the Augsburg Confession of 1530, a foundational document of Lutheranism. This confession became the basis for the formation of the Lutheran Church. Lutheranism spread to other parts of Europe, with regions such as Scandinavia adopting it as their official faith.

Martin Luther's impact on the world was profound. His reform movement led to the fragmentation of Western Christianity, with the emergence of various Protestant denominations. His emphasis on the authority of Scripture, justification by faith, and the priesthood of all believers laid the groundwork for the development of modern Protestantism. Luther's translation of the Bible into the vernacular languages also played a crucial role in shaping the languages and cultures of Europe.

Martin Luther's life was a testament to the power of an individual who stood firm in his beliefs, even in the face of immense pressure and opposition. His legacy endures in the form of Protestantism, which has become one of the major branches of Christianity, and his impact on theology, education, and the world at large cannot be overstated. Martin Luther's life and work continue to be a subject of fascination and inspiration for people around the world.

Major Ideas and Philosophy of Martin Luther

Martin Luther's works and philosophy were instrumental in shaping the Protestant Reformation and had a profound impact on theology, religion, and society. Here are some major ideas from his works and philosophy:

JUSTIFICATION BY FAITH ALONE (SOLA FIDE): Martin Luther's central doctrine of justification by faith alone, known as "sola fide," was a revolutionary concept in the 16th century. Luther's emphasis on faith underscored that salvation is not attained through mere good works or adherence to Church rituals but is a free gift of God's grace. He believed that individuals could be justified and reconciled with God by placing their trust in Jesus Christ's atonement for their sins. This teaching not only liberated believers from the burden of earning their salvation through their own deeds but also gave them a profound sense of assurance, rooted in God's faithfulness rather than human merit.

JOYFUL AND PARTICIPATORY WORSHIP: Martin Luther was a proponent of a more joyful and participatory form of worship. He believed that Christian worship should be a celebration of faith and an expression of the believer's joy in God's grace. In contrast to the often solemn and fearful tone of Catholic worship during the Middle Ages, Luther encouraged a more uplifting and communal experience. Luther's emphasis on congregational singing, including the creation of hymns in the vernacular language, allowed ordinary people to actively participate in the worship service. He believed that singing hymns and praises in the language of the people not only made worship more accessible but also fostered a sense of unity and joy within the congregation. These ideas and principles remain integral to the theological foundations of various Protestant denominations and have had a lasting impact on the broader Christian tradition and Western culture.

SOLA SCRIPTURA: Luther's principle of "sola scriptura" centered on the supreme authority of the Bible in matters of faith and practice. He argued that the Scriptures alone should serve as the ultimate source of religious truth, guiding the beliefs and practices of the Church. Luther's translation of the Bible into German further empowered the common people, as it made the Bible accessible in their vernacular language. This move democratized religious knowledge, enabling individuals to read and interpret the Scriptures for themselves, and had a lasting impact on religious thought and literacy.

PRIESTHOOD OF ALL BELIEVERS: Luther challenged the prevailing notion of a hierarchical clergy by introducing the concept of the "priesthood of all believers." According to this doctrine, every believer had a direct and personal relationship with God, eliminating the need for intermediaries like priests to connect with the divine. This concept not only emphasized the universal access to God but also empowered the laity to pray, study the Bible, and engage in worship and ministry on a personal level. It shifted the dynamics of religious practice and the roles of individuals within the Church.

OPPOSITION TO INDULGENCES: Martin Luther's vehement opposition to the sale of indulgences by the Catholic Church stemmed from his perception of their corruption and abuse. Indulgences were a controversial practice within the Catholic Church, offering remission of the temporal punishment for sins, often in exchange for acts of penance or monetary offerings. Luther believed that the sale of indulgences exploited people's fear of divine punishment and distorted the true message of God's grace. This opposition led Luther to write his famous "95 Theses," which he publicly posted, inviting a debate on the practice. This act would become the catalyst for the Protestant Reformation, challenging the status quo and setting off a religious revolution.

THE THEOLOGY OF THE CROSS: Luther's "theology of the cross" was a theological framework that emphasized the redemptive significance of Christ's suffering and crucifixion. It contrasted with the prevailing "theology of glory," which celebrated human achievements, worldly success, and outward displays of power. The theology of the cross challenged believers to embrace the paradox of faith, where God's strength was revealed in what appeared to be weakness. This perspective encouraged a deeper understanding of the Christian faith that acknowledged the role of suffering and difficulties in life, ultimately influencing how people viewed the Christian journey.

TWO KINGDOMS DOCTRINE: Luther's "two kingdoms" doctrine was a theological framework that posited the existence of two distinct realms —the earthly and the heavenly—each governed by God but with different modes of governance. In the earthly realm, Luther recognized the authority of secular governments and institutions, while in the heavenly realm, he acknowledged God's sovereignty over spiritual matters. This idea had significant implications for the relationship between the Church and the state. Luther encouraged Christians to be active and responsible citizens in both realms, recognizing that God's presence and principles should guide their actions in the world without necessitating theocratic rule. This doctrine contributed to the development of ideas about the separation of church and state and religious freedom.

MARRIAGE AS A VOCATION: Luther's own marriage to Katharina von Bora challenged the prevailing notion of celibacy among the clergy. Luther believed that marriage was a legitimate and honorable vocation, and he viewed it as a reflection of God's design for human relationships. By marrying and advocating for the right of clergy to marry, Luther not only challenged the practices of enforced celibacy within the Catholic Church but also emphasized the sacredness of the marital union. This stance had a profound influence on the understanding of marriage within Christian traditions and contributed to discussions on the role of family life within the Church.

WORSHIP IN THE VERNACULAR: One of Martin Luther's significant reforms was advocating for religious services to be conducted in the vernacular language of the people rather than in Latin, which was the traditional language of worship in the Catholic Church. By making worship accessible to the common person in their native language, Luther aimed to emphasize understanding and active participation in the liturgy. This shift had a democratizing effect on religious practice, as it enabled congregants to engage more fully in the worship experience. It not only brought the Word of God closer to the people but also allowed them to personally connect with and comprehend the theological content of the services.

EDUCATIONAL REFORMS: Martin Luther held a deep commitment to education and believed in the importance of promoting literacy and religious learning. He recognized that the ability to read the Bible and engage with religious texts was essential for individuals to form a personal relationship with God. To this end, Luther established schools and encouraged the development of an educational system that would ensure that people could access the Scriptures and become literate. His efforts laid the foundation for the creation of Protestant educational institutions in various regions, thereby advancing knowledge, religious understanding, and literacy among the general populace.

SOCIAL AND POLITICAL INFLUENCE: Martin Luther's ideas were not confined to matters of faith but had significant political and social implications. His emphasis on individual conscience and religious freedom paved the way for principles of religious tolerance and freedom of conscience in later centuries. Luther's willingness to challenge authority, both within the Church and in the political realm, encouraged others to question established hierarchies and contributed to the broader movements for religious and political reform. His writings and beliefs played a pivotal role in shaping the events of his time and had a lasting impact on the development of democratic and religiously pluralistic societies.

Martin Luther's ideas and philosophy left an indelible mark on the course of history. His theological contributions and social reforms continue to influence religious thought and the broader understanding of individual and collective faith. Luther's legacy as a reformer, theologian, and advocate for religious freedom endures to this day, shaping the beliefs and practices of millions around the world.

Faith is the
'yes' of the heart,
a conviction on
which one stakes
one's life.

I did not learn my theology all at once, but had to search constantly deeper and deeper for it. My temptations did that for me, for no one can understand Holy Scripture without practice and temptations...It is not by reading, writing, or speculation that one becomes a theologian. Nay, rather, it is living, dying, and being damned that makes one a theologian.

The prosperity of a country depends, not on the abundance of its revenues, nor on the strength of its fortifications, nor on the beauty of its public buildings; but it consists in the number of its cultivated citizens, in its men of education, enlightenment and character.

God is not a God of sadness, death, etc., but the devil is. Christ is a God of joy, and so the Scriptures often say that we should rejoice ... A Christian should and must be a cheerful person.

The kingdom of God does not consist in talk, but in power, that is, in works and practice. God loves the 'doers of the word' in faith and love, and not the 'mere hearers,' who, like parrots, have learned to utter certain expressions with readiness.

Whoever does not
know God hidden in
suffering does not
know God at all.

Faith ever says,
"If Thou wilt,"
not "If Thou canst."

One ought to fast, watch, and labor to the extent that such activities are needed to harness the body's desires and longings; however, those who presume that they are justified by works pay no attention to the need for self-discipline but see the works themselves as the way to righteousness. They believe that if they do a great number of impressive works all will be well and righteousness will be the result. Sometimes this is pursued with such zeal that they become mentally unstable and their bodies are sapped of all strength. Such disastrous consequences demonstrate that the belief that we are justified and saved by works without faith is extremely foolish.

Unless I am convicted by Scripture and plain reason —I do not accept the authority of popes and councils, for they have contradicted each other—my conscience is captive to the Word of God. I cannot and will not recant anything, for to go against conscience is neither right nor safe. Here I stand, I cannot do otherwise. God help me. Amen.

Holy Christendom has, in my judgment, no better teacher after the apostles than St. Augustine.

For where God built a church, there the Devil would also build a chapel... Thus is the Devil ever God's ape.

When God works in us, the will, being changed and sweetly breathed upon by the Spirit of God, desires and acts, not from compulsion, but responsively.

O, when it comes to faith, what a living, creative, active, powerful thing it is. It cannot do other than good at all times. It never waits to ask whether there is some good work to do...

Whenever the devil harasses you, seek the company of men or drink more, or joke and talk nonsense, or do some other merry thing. Sometimes we must drink more, sport, recreate ourselves, and even sin a little to spite the devil, so that we leave him no place for troubling our consciences with trifles. We are conquered if we try too conscientiously not to sin at all. So when the devil says to you: do not drink, answer him: I will drink, and right freely, just because you tell me not to.

There is no more
lovely, friendly and
charming relationship,
communion or company
than a good marriage.

Power without love is
reckless and abusive,
and love without power
is sentimental
and anemic.

The mad mob does not ask how it could be better, only that it be different. And when it then becomes worse, it must change again. Thus they get bees for flies, and at last hornets for bees.

A Christian lives not in himself, but in Christ and in his neighbor. Otherwise he is not a Christian. He lives in Christ through faith, in his neighbor through love.

By faith he is caught up beyond himself into God. By love he descends beneath himself into his neighbor.

A just law is a man-made code that squares with the moral law or the law of God. An unjust law is a code that is out of harmony with the moral law. To put it in the terms of Saint Thomas Aquinas, an unjust law is a human law that is not rooted in eternal and natural law.

Tell your master that if there were as many devils at Worms as tiles on its roofs, I would enter.

(On the 16th of April, 1521, Luther entered the imperial city [of Worms]... On his approach... the Elector's chancellor entreated him, in the name of his master, not to enter a town where his death was decided. The answer which Luther returned was simply this.)

Faith is a living, bold trust in God's grace, so certain of God's favor that it would risk death a thousand times trusting in it. Such confidence and knowledge of God's grace makes you happy, joyful and bold in your relationship to God and all creatures. The Holy Spirit makes this happen through faith. Because of it, you freely, willingly and joyfully do good to everyone, serve everyone, suffer all kinds of things, love and praise the God who has shown you such grace.

The Bible is the proper book for men. There the truth is distinguished from error far more clearly than anywhere else, and one finds something new in it every day. For 28 years, since I became a doctor, I have now constantly read and preached the Bible; and yet I have not exhausted it but find something new in it every day.

No man understands the Scriptures, unless he be acquainted with the Cross.

Not only the words (vocabula) which the Holy Spirit and Scripture use are divine, but also the phrasing.

Singing has nothing to do with the affairs of this world: it is not for the law. Singers are merry, and free from sorrows and cares.

I know God only as
he became human,
so shall I have him
in no other way.

Heavy thoughts
bring on physical
maladies; when the
soul is oppressed
so is the body.

When the devil comes at night to worry me, this is what I say to him: Devil, I have to sleep now. That is God's commandment, for us to work by day and sleep at night. If he keeps on nagging me and trots out my sins, then I answer: Sweet devil, I know the whole list. But I have done even more sin which is not on your list. Write there also that I have shit in my breeches. Hang it around your neck and wipe your mouth on it. Then, if he won't cease to accuse me of sins, I say in contempt:
Holy Satan, pray for me.
("Sancte Satane, ora pro me")

God the Almighty has made our rulers mad; they actually think they can do—and order their subjects to do—whatever they please. And the subjects make the mistake of believing that they, in turn, are bound to obey their rulers in everything.

May a merciful God preserve me from a Christian Church in which everyone is a saint! I want to be and remain in the church and little flock of the fainthearted, the feeble and the ailing, who feel and recognize the wretchedness of their sins, who sigh and cry to God incessantly for comfort and help, who believe in the forgiveness of sins.

We need to pledge ourselves anew to the cause of Christ. We must capture the spirit of the early church. Wherever the early Christians went, they made a triumphant witness for Christ. Whether on the village streets or in the city jails, they daringly proclaimed the good news of the gospel.

What does it mean to have a god? or, what is God? Answer: A god means that from which we are to expect all good and to which we are to take refuge in all distress, so that to have a God is nothing else than to trust and believe Him from the [whole] heart; as I have often said that the confidence and faith of the heart alone make both God and an idol. If your faith and trust be right, then is your god also true; and, on the other hand, if your trust be false and wrong, then you have not the true God; for these two belong together faith and God. That now, I say, upon which you set your heart and put your trust is properly your god.

The believing man hath the Holy Ghost; and where the Holy Ghost dwelleth, He will not suffer a man to be idle, but stirreth him up to all exercises of piety and godliness, and of true religion, to the love of God, to the patient suffering of afflictions, to prayer, to thanksgiving, and the exercise of charity towards all men.

Be a sinner and sin
strongly, but more
strongly have faith
and rejoice in Christ.

By faith we began,
by hope we continue,
and by revelation
we shall obtain
the whole.

A great variety of reading confuses and does not teach. It makes the student like a man who dwells everywhere and, therefore, nowhere in particular.

I would take to be quite a fool any man who would make a book full of laws and statutes for an apple tree telling it how to bear apples and not thorns, when the tree is able by its own nature to do this better than the man with all his books can describe and demand.

A person must take care to exercise moderate discipline over the body and subject it to the Spirit by means of fasting, vigils, and labor. The goal is to have the body obey and conform — and not hinder — the inner person and faith. Unless it is held in check, we know it is the nature of the body to undermine faith and the inner person.

Superstition, idolatry, and hypocrisy have ample wages, but truth goes a-begging.

What is sought by means of free choice is to make room for merits.

As concerning faith we ought to be invincible, and more hard, if it might be, than the adamant stone; but as touching charity, we ought to be soft, and more flexible than the reed or leaf that is shaken with the wind, and ready to yield to everything.

To serve God is nothing else than to serve your neighbor and do good to him in love, be it a child, wife, servant, enemy, friend....If you do not find yourself among the needy and the poor, where the Gospel shows us Christ, then you may know that your faith is not right, and that you have not yet tasted of Christ's benevolence and work for you.

From the beginning of my Reformation I have asked God to send me neither dreams, nor visions, nor angels, but to give me the right understanding of His Word, the Holy Scriptures; for as long as I have God's Word, I know that I am walking in His way and that I shall not fall into any error or delusion.

God wants us to pray, and he wants to hear our prayers— not because we are worthy, but because he is merciful.

The bible is a remarkable fountain: the more one draws and drinks of it, the more it stimulates thirst.

I think these things [firearms] were invented by Satan himself, for they can't be defended against with (ordinary) weapons and fists. All human strength vanishes when confronted with firearms. A man is dead before he sees what's coming.

Our preaching does not stop with the law. That would lead to wounding without binding up, striking down and not healing, killing and not making alive, driving down to hell and not bringing back up, humbling and not exalting. Therefore, we must also preach grace and the promise of forgiveness—this is the means by which faith is awakened and properly taught. Without this word of grace, the law, contrition, penitence, and everything else are done and taught in vain.

A Christian is free and independent in every respect, a bond servant to none.

A Christian is a dutiful servant in every respect, owing a duty to everyone.

If you are a preacher of mercy, do not preach an imaginary but the true mercy. If the mercy is true, you must therefore bear the true, not an imaginary sin.

This is the most dangerous trial of all, when there is no trial and every thing goes well; for then a man is tempted to forget God, to become too bold and to misuse times of prosperity.

If obedience is not rendered in the homes, we shall never have a whole city, country, principality, or kingdom well governed. For this order in the homes is the first rule; it is the source of all other rule and government.

The highest and most precious treasure we receive of God is, that we can speak, hear, see, etc.; but how few acknowledge these as God's special gifts, much less give God thanks for them.

I am persuaded that without knowledge of literature pure theology cannot at all endure.... When letters have declined and lain prostrate, theology, too, has wretchedly fallen and lain prostrate.... It is my desire that there shall be as many poets and rhetoricians as possible, because I see that by these studies as by no other means, people are wonderfully fitted for the grasping of sacred truth and for handling it skillfully and happily.

How rich a God our God is! He gives enough, but we don't notice it. He gave the whole world to Adam, but this was nothing in Adam's eyes; he was concerned about one tree and had to ask why God had forbidden him to eat it.

The great unthankfulness, contempt of God's word, and wilfulness of the world, make me fear that the divine light will soon cease to shine on man, for God's word has ever had its certain course.

At night always carry in your heart something from Holy Scriptures to bed with you, meditate upon it like a ruminant animal, and go softly to sleep; but this must not be too much, rather a little that may be well pondered and understood, that you may find a remnant of it in your mind when you rise in the morning.

The more a person loves, the closer he approaches the image of God.

... a penny saved is better than a penny earned.

It is a good thing to let prayer be the first business in the morning and the last in the evening. Guard yourself against such false and deceitful thoughts that keep whispering, "Wait a while. In an hour or so I will pray. I must first finish this or that." Thinking such thoughts we get away from prayer into other things that will hold us and involve us till the prayer of the day comes to naught.

It is the part of a Christian to take care of his own body for the very purpose that by its soundness and well being he may be enabled to labour... for the aid of those who are in want, that thus the stronger member may serve the weaker member, and we may be children of God, and busy for one another, bearing one another's burdens, and so fulfilling the law of Christ.

Heaven and earth, all the emperors, kings, and princes of the world, could not raise a fit dwelling-place for God; yet, in a weak human soul, that keeps His Word, He willingly resides.

What can only be taught by the rod and with blows will not lead to much good; they will not remain pious any longer than the rod is behind them.

The Bible is the book that makes fools of the wise of this world; it is only understood by the plain and simple hearted.

The devil and temptations also do give occasion unto us somewhat to learn and understand the Scriptures, by experience and practice. Without trials and temptations we should never understand anything thereof; no, not although we diligently read and heard the same.

So it is with human
reason, which strives
not against faith,
when enlightened,
but rather furthers
and advances it.

To comfort a sorrowful conscience is much better than to possess many kingdoms; yet the world regards it not; nay, condemns it, calling us rebels, disturbers of the peace.

Unto him who is able to keep us from falling, and lift us from the dark to the bright mountain of hope, from the midnight of desperation to the daybreak of joy, to him be power and authority for ever and ever.

For some years now I have read through the Bible twice every year. If you picture the Bible to be a mighty tree and every word a little branch, I have shaken every one of these branches because I wanted to know what it was and what it meant.

None can believe how powerful prayer is, and what it is able to effect, but those who have learned it by experience.

The heavenly blessing is to be delivered from the law, sin and death; to be justified and quickened to life: to have peace with God; to have a faithful heart, a joyful conscience, a spiritual consolation; to have the knowledge of Jesus Christ; to have the gift of prophecy, and the revelation of the Scriptures; to have the gift of the Holy Ghost, and to rejoice in God.

By God's grace, I know Satan very well. If Satan can turn God's Word upside down and pervert the Scriptures, what will he do with my words -- or the words of others?

Adam was created righteous, acceptable, and without sin. He had no need from his labor in the garden to be made righteous and acceptable to God. Rather, the Lord gave Adam work in order to cultivate and protect the garden. This would have been the freest of all works because they were done simply to please God and not to obtain righteousness. ... The works of the person who trusts God are to be understood in a similar manner. Through faith we are restored to paradise and created anew. We have no need of works in order to be righteous; however, in order to avoid idleness and so that the body might be cared for an disciplined, works are done freely to please God.

God delights in our temptations and yet hates them. He delights in them when they drive us to prayer; he hates them when they drive us to despair.

I ask that people make no reference to my name; let them call themselves Christians, not Lutherans. What is Luther? After all, the teaching is not mine. Neither was I crucified for anyone. St. Paul, in I Corinthians 3, would not allow the Christians to call themselves Pauline or Petrine but Christian. How then should I - poor stinking maggot-fodder than I am - come to have people call the children of Christ by my wretched name? Not so, my dear friends; let us abolish all party names and call ourselves Christian.

A fiery shield is God's Word; of more substance and purer than gold, which, tried in the fire, loses nought of its substance, but resists and overcomes all the fury of the fiery heat; even so, he that believes God's Word overcomes all, and remains secure everlastingly, against all misfortunes; for this shield fears nothing, neither hell nor the devil.

This life therefore is not righteousness, but growth in righteousness, not health, but healing, not being but becoming, not rest but exercise. We are not yet what we shall be, but we are growing toward it, the process is not yet finished, but it is going on, this is not the end, but it is the road. All does not yet gleam in glory, but all is being purified.

Music is one of the fairest and most glorious gifts of God, to which Satan is a bitter enemy; for it removes from the heart the weight of sorrow, and the fascination of evil thoughts.

There can be no be no better instruction... than that every man who is to deal with his neighbor to follow these commandments. 'Whatsoever ye would that others should do unto you, do ye also unto them,' and 'Love thy neighbor as thyself.' If these were always followed, then everything would instruct and arrange itself; then no law books nor courts nor judicial actions would be required. All things would quietly and simply be set to rights, for everyone's heart and conscience would guide them.

This grace of God is a very great, strong, mighty and active thing. It does not lie asleep in the soul. Grace hears, leads, drives, draws, changes, works all in man, and lets itself be distinctly felt and experienced. It is hidden, but its works are evident.

When the devil wants to cause offense against the true doctrine and faith, he does not do so through insignificant people, who do not rate highly with the world, but through those who are the very best, the wisest, the holiest, and the most learned.

Dear rulers ... I maintain that the civil authorities are under obligation to compel the people to send their children to school. ... If the government can compel such citizens as are fit for military service to bear spear and rifle, to mount ramparts, and perform other martial duties in time of war, how much more has it a right to compel the people to send their children to school, because in this case we are warring with the devil, whose object it is secretly to exhaust our cities and principalities of their strong men.

I admit that I deserve death and hell, what of it? For I know One who suffered and made satisfaction on my behalf. His name is Jesus Christ, Son of God, and where He is there I shall be also!

Faith looks to the word and the promise; that is, to the truth. But hope looks to that which the word has promised, to the gift.

Here is the truly Christian life, here is faith really working by love, when a man applies himself with joy and love to the works of that freest servitude in which he serves others voluntarily and for nought, himself abundantly satisfied in the fullness and riches of his own faith.

It is certainly true that reason is the most important and the highest rank among all things and, in comparison with other things of this life, the best and something divine. It is the inventor and mentor of all the arts, medicines, laws, and of whatever wisdom, power, virtue, and glory men possess in this life.

He who loves not
women, wine, and song
Remains a fool his
whole life long.

True Christian love
is not derived from
things without, but
floweth from the
heart, as from a
spring.

Leave the ass burdened with laws behind in the valley. But your conscience, let it ascend with Isaac into the mountain.

Our stubbornness is right, because we want to preserve the liberty which we have in Christ. Only by preserving our liberty shall we be able to retain the truth of the Gospel inviolate.

God is ready to give more quickly, and to give more than you ask; yea, he offers his treasures if we only take them. It is truly a great shame and a severe chastisement for us Christians that God should still upbraid us for our slothfulness in prayer, and that we fail to let such a rich and excellent promise incite us to pray.

If there is anything in us, it is not our own; it is a gift of God. But if it is a gift of God, then it is entirely a debt one owes to love, that is, to the law of Christ. And if it is a debt owed to love, then I must serve others with it, not myself.

We may search long to find where God is, but we shall find Him in those who keep the words of Christ. For the Lord Christ saith, " If any man love me, he will keep my words; and we will make our abode with him."

A preacher must be both soldier and shepherd. He must nourish, defend, and teach; he must have teeth in his mouth, and be able to bite and fight.

My learning is not my own; it belongs to the unlearned and is the debt I owe them...
My wisdom belongs to the foolish, my power to the oppressed.
Thus my wealth belongs to the poor, my righteousness to the sinners...

Faith, like light, should ever be simple and unbending; while love, like warmth, should beam forth on every side, and bend to every necessity of our brethren.

The Apostle Paul wants us to work with our hands in order to share with the needy (Ephesians 5:28). Notice that he could have said that we should work to support ourselves. But Paul says that we work to give to those in need. This is why caring for our body is also a Christian work. If the body is healthy and fit, we are able to work and save money that can be used to help those in need.

When speaking of the spiritual nature or the soul, we are referring to that which is "inner" or "new." When speaking of the bodily nature, or that which is flesh and blood, we are referring to that which is called "sensual," "outward," or "old." Paul writes in 2 Corinthians 4:16: "Even though our outer nature is wasting away, our inner nature is being renewed day by day."

We refuse to have our conscience bound by any work or law, so that by doing this or that we should be righteous, or leaving this or that undone we should be damned.

We must make a great difference between God's Word and the word of man. A man's word is a little sound, that flies into the air, and soon vanishes; but the Word of God is greater than heaven and earth, yea, greater than death and hell, for it forms part of the power of God, and endures everlastingly.

Christ ought to be preached with this goal in mind—that we might be moved to faith in him so that he is not just a distant historical figure but actually Christ for you and me.

Peace is more important than all justice; and peace was not made for the sake of justice, but justice for the sake of peace.

Take a look at your own heart, and you will soon find out what has stuck to it and where your treasure is. It is easy to determine whether hearing the Word of God, living according to it, and achieving such a life gives you as much enjoyment and calls forth as much diligence from you as does accumulating and saving money and property.

I am of a different mind ten times in the course of a day. But I resist the devil, and often it is with a fart that I chase him away. When he tempts me with silly sins I say, 'Devil, yesterday I broke wind too. Have you written it down on your list?

Sleep is a most useful and most salutary operation of nature. Scarcely any minor annoyance angers me more than the being suddenly awakened out of a pleasant slumber. I understand that in Italy they torture poor people by depriving them of sleep. Tis a torture that cannot long be endured.

It is the nature of all hypocrites and false prophets to create a conscience where there is none, and to cause conscience to disappear where it does exist.

Man is by nature unable to want God to be God. Indeed, he himself wants to be God, and does not want God to be God.

True humility does not know that it is humble. If it did, it would be proud from the contemplation of so fine a virtue.